UNSOLVED MYSTERIES

The Disappearance of Amelia Earhart

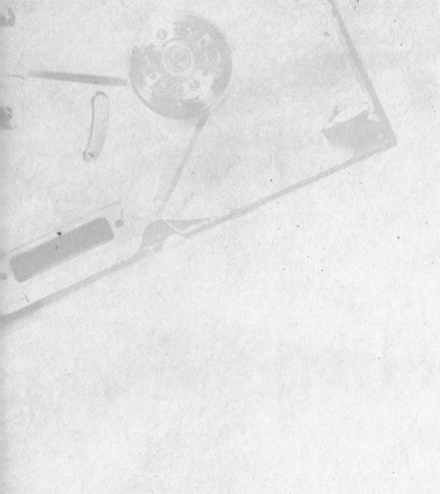

ABDO
Publishing Company

The Disappearance of Amelia Earhart

By A. M. Buckley

Content Consultant
David Jourdan
Founder and President,
Nauticos

CREDITS

Published by ABDO Publishing Company, PO Box 398166, Minneapolis, MN 55439. Copyright © 2012 by Abdo Consulting Group, Inc. International copyrights reserved in all countries. No part of this book may be reproduced in any form without written permission from the publisher. The Essential Library™ is a trademark and logo of ABDO Publishing Company.

Printed in the United States of America,
North Mankato, Minnesota
102011
012012

Editor: Melissa York
Copy Editor: Kathryn-Ann Geis
Series design: Becky Daum, Christa Schneider, & Ellen Schofield
Cover and interior production: Christa Schneider

Library of Congress Cataloging-in-Publication Data
Buckley, A. M., 1968-
  The disappearance of Amelia Earhart / by A.M. Buckley.
    p. cm. -- (Unsolved mysteries)
  Includes bibliographical references.
  ISBN 978-1-61783-302-1
  1. Earhart, Amelia, 1897-1937--Death and burial--Juvenile literature. 2. Air pilots--United States--Death--Juvenile literature. 3. Aircraft accidents--Investigation--Juvenile literature. I. Title.
  TL540.E3B83 2012
  629.13092--dc23
                                        2011034605

Table of Contents

Chapter 1

Scanning the Sky

On June 1, 1937, world-famous flyer Amelia Earhart set off with her navigator, Fred Noonan, on a journey around the world. They were crammed into her small but powerful airplane, a Lockheed Electra. If they completed their journey, Earhart would be the first woman to manage the feat.

Earhart's Electra, a twin-engine Lockheed plane capable of cruising at 200 miles per hour (320 km/h), cost $80,000 by the time it was fitted with state-of-the-art equipment.

A month and a day later, having traveled almost all the way around the world, Earhart and Noonan took off on the most difficult leg of their long flight. The tired but courageous aviator flew through the night, aiming her plane toward Howland Island, a tiny piece of land in the Pacific Ocean that had been designated as her next-to-last stop.

It was not an easy island to spot from the air, even for expert navigator Noonan, but the Electra made its way confidently through the night skies, heading for Howland.

International Acclaim

Amelia Earhart was a huge celebrity in her day. Crowds of hundreds, even thousands, came to see her off on her record-breaking journeys. After the successful landing of her historic 1932 solo flight across the Atlantic, she received telegrams from friends and family but also from heads of state from around the world, dignitaries, aviators, and other well-wishers proud of her accomplishment.

Throughout her career, she continued to break records and earn the respect of fans. But flying was expensive, and for each new adventure she needed to raise money for the airplane, fuel, and other equipment. To that end, Earhart gave lectures and interviews, wrote books and articles, and even started a line of clothing and luggage. These ventures helped her earn money for her first love, flying.

Earhart was generous with her time and passion for aviation. She believed wholeheartedly in the possibilities of airline travel before it was common or considered safe, and she spoke eloquently about equal rights for all. Earhart's bravery, accomplishments, and grace under pressure added to her mounting and widespread acclaim, which has only grown since her mysterious disappearance.

Ready for Arrival

One year before Earhart's scheduled landing, US President Franklin D. Roosevelt had issued a memorandum approving the construction of three runways on Howland Island. The purpose of the runways was not specifically outlined, but the order was preceded by a request from Earhart, a friend of

Earhart's projects were made possible by the support of Eleanor Roosevelt, *far left*, and President Franklin D. Roosevelt, *far right*. Earhart is second from the left.

the First Lady and
a supporter of the
president, asking
for a landing site for
her round-the-world
attempt.

The airfield was
completed at a cost of
$9,981, courtesy of
the US government.

DIRECTION FINDER: A direction-finding radio receiver is capable of determining the direction, or bearing, from which a signal is being sent. It was a relatively new technology at the time of the Earhart flight and operated best at low frequencies. A high-frequency direction finder, able to operate at high frequencies, was set up on Howland Island as a backup measure.

In the early morning hours of July 1, 1937, three
bare, white-sand landing strips glinted in the
moonlight, ready for the arrival of the first plane ever
to touch down on the small island.

Frank Cipriani, radioman 2nd class with the
US Coast Guard, was waiting on the beach. He was
charged with the operation of an experimental, high-frequency direction finder, borrowed from the navy
to provide support for Earhart's flight.

Offshore, Commander Warner K. Thompson of
the Coast Guard ship *Itasca* and his crew were also
waiting for the Electra. The ship had been tasked
with supporting the flight. They would refuel the
plane upon landing, but before that, they would
relay weather and other vital information to the pilot
as she made her way to Howland.

Earhart consults a map with her navigator, Fred Noonan.

Radio Communication

The radio room, a small area on the top deck, was
the busiest section of the ship that early morning
in July. Chief Radioman Leo G. Bellarts supervised
both the radio operators on board and Cipriani on
the beach. Bellarts and his team listened attentively
for messages from the Earhart plane. The floor
and walls of the Radio Room were filled with large
metal cabinets that held the ship's vital equipment
for transmitting and receiving messages on the

radio. Squeezed between the cabinets were two desks for the radio operators, each outfitted with a telegraph key, used for sending Morse code, and a typewriter, used to keep a log of heard and received messages.

Itasca radio operators wore headphones to listen to voice messages, which were sent across the airwaves on radio frequencies. Voice messages could also be broadcast throughout the room on a speaker mounted on one wall.

At 2:30 a.m., Bellarts sent a

Radio Waves

From the 1920s through the 1950s, Americans gathered around the radio to listen to stories in much the same way they now watch television. Radio was also a primary means of wireless communication and was used to help planes and ships navigate.

Radios work by transmitting signals as sound waves. The waves pass from a transmitter through an antenna, which broadcasts the signals through the air. In order for these sounds to be heard, the receiver must be set at the same frequency as the transmitter. Just as you tune a car radio to get a particular station, people communicating via radio need to be on the same channel. Frequencies are measured in kilohertz. High numbers indicate a high-frequency signal, and low numbers indicate a low-frequency signal.

Earhart's Electra had three radio antennae. One ran from front to back on the top of the plane in a *V* shape; this was used to transmit, or send, signals. The main antenna used to receive signals ran along the belly, or bottom, of the plane. A secondary receiving antenna, shaped like a loop, was located inside the cockpit. A nearby switch allowed the pilot to choose which receiving antenna to use at any time.

message to the Electra, "Itasca to Earhart."[1] At 2:45 a.m., Bellarts heard the first radio message from

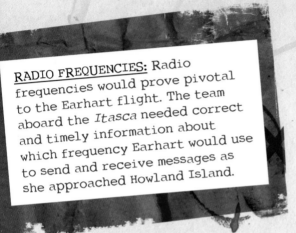

RADIO FREQUENCIES: Radio frequencies would prove pivotal to the Earhart flight. The team aboard the *Itasca* needed correct and timely information about which frequency Earhart would use to send and receive messages as she approached Howland Island.

Earhart. But the signal was weak, and he was unable to decipher the message. In his log, Bellarts wrote, "Heard Earhart plane but unreadable thru static."[2]

For the next several hours, Bellarts and his team listened attentively but heard only intermittent and terse messages from the plane. They also transmitted messages at regular intervals. But as Earhart's estimated time of arrival edged closer, they had yet to establish two-way radio communication with the plane.

To land safely, Earhart would need weather information from the ship as well as verification of the island's location. As the sun rose over the sea, there was no news of the flight. The atmosphere on the *Itasca* was thick with tension.

The Coast Guard ship *Itasca*, bottom, ran on fuel oil and could travel at 16 nautical miles per hour (30 km/h).

No Sign of the Plane

Earhart's husband and publicist, George Palmer Putnam, was in California. With the help of members of the Coast Guard, he tried desperately to relay information about the flight that might help the *Itasca* make radio contact with his wife. In Washington DC, President Roosevelt and the First Lady awoke to a new day only to learn the US Coast Guard had yet to send a message to the plane, and

TRANSATLANTIC FLIGHT: The first person to fly across the Atlantic Ocean was the famous aviator Charles Lindbergh in May 1927. His historic flight earned the pilot international fame and the nickname Lucky Lindy. Earhart achieved a similar level of fame and the nickname Lady Lindy after becoming the first woman to cross the Atlantic as an airplane passenger in June 1928. She became the second person and first woman to fly solo across the Atlantic in May 1932.

communications from the plane had stopped. Earhart was missing.

In the coming days, the government would mount a massive rescue mission in search of Earhart and Noonan. The 16-day search involved 4,000 men, ten ships, and 65 airplanes.

Putnam and other friends of Earhart and Noonan listened hopefully to the news of scattered radio transmissions reportedly heard from various spots in the United States. Putnam sought the help of psychics and wrote multiple letters to the government, expressing gratitude while requesting additional help.

But the biggest rescue mission in US history came up empty-handed. On July 19, 1937, the US Navy completed the search for Earhart and Noonan. No sign of the pilot, navigator, or plane was found then or has been discovered since.

DAILY NEWS FINAL

NEW YORK'S ★ PICTURE NEWSPAPER

Copyright 1937 by News Syndi-
cate Co., Inc. Reg. U.S. Pat. Off.

Entered as 2nd class matter,
Post Office, New York, N. Y.

New York, Saturday, July 3, 1937*

Vol. 19. No. 6   28 Pages   2 Cents IN CITY | 3 CENTS LIMITS | Elsewhere

EARHART PLANE LOST AT SEA

Story on Page 3

Amelia Earhart Missing on World Flight

· Evidently overshooting their mark, Amelia Earhart and Fred Noonan (left), her navigator, were believed down in the Pacific near lonely Howland Island, on 2,550-mile hop from Lae, New Guinea. Friends thought ship would float for some time. This picture was made at Karachi, India, as the two fliers were greeted by Viscount Sibour (right) on arrival there on globe-girdling flight. —Story on page 3.

(By Wide World)

Newspapers around the country quickly reported Earhart's disappearance.

Chapter 2

A Girl Born to Fly

Amelia Mary Earhart was born on July 24, 1897, in Atchison, Kansas, to parents Amy and Edwin Earhart. Amelia spent the first few months of her life with her mother and extended family in the large and comfortable home of her grandparents, Amelia and Alfred Otis. That fall, Amelia's mother brought her daughter to Kansas City, Missouri, where Edwin had a job working for the railroad. In Kansas City, the young parents struggled to make ends meet. Throughout her childhood, Amelia would return to the house in Atchison for much of the year, spending summers in Kansas City with her parents.

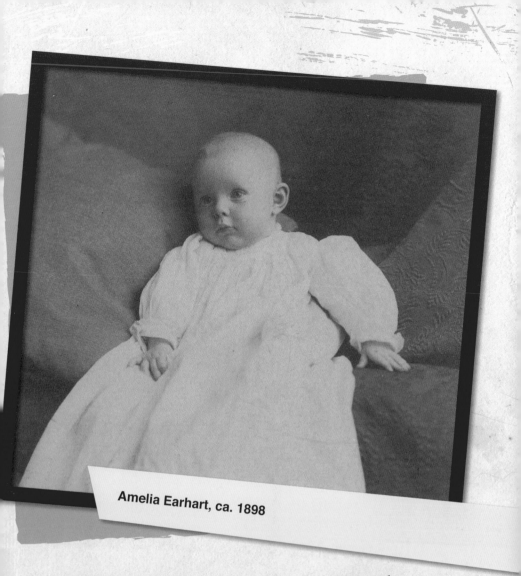

Amelia Earhart, ca. 1898

Amelia and her younger sister, Grace Muriel Earhart, called Muriel, attended classes at the College Preparatory School in Atchison. A report by headmistress Sarah Walton noted that Amelia "deduces the correct answer to complex arithmetic problems but hates to put down the steps by which she arrives at the results."[1]

At a young age, Amelia already displayed the confidence and charm of the woman she would become.

Amelia was fond of adventure from a young age. She loved to play outdoors with her sister and cousins and was a leader among the neighborhood children. One of her favorite activities was to jump the fence around the house. Amelia's grandmother was a woman of her times and expected her girls to behave like young ladies. Learning of Amelia's play, her grandmother told her, "Ladies don't climb fences, child. Only boys do that. Little girls use the gate."[2]

Ahead of Her Time

Despite her grandmother's aims to keep her indoors and in dresses, Amelia remained interested in the sorts of daring and adventurous activities normally reserved for boys. In addition to climbing fences, she played baseball, rode bicycles, and greatly enjoyed caring for and riding horses. Amelia seemed neither to understand nor agree with the idea that girls should behave any differently than boys.

Throughout childhood and adolescence, Amelia demonstrated on several occasions that she was not terribly concerned about rules or authority. She tended to act on her own principles rather than according to any code set by family, school, or society.

As she grew from childhood to adolescence, changes in her life and character added to the picture of the woman she would become and perhaps nurtured her independent spirit. She was still adventurous but developed another, reflective side. She began writing poetry, a habit she would continue throughout her life. She also kept private scrapbooks, archiving newspaper articles about women's achievements, perhaps hoping one day to add her own name to the list of these early pioneers.

AN INDEPENDENT STREAK: Some speculate that it was Amelia's independent spirit, her tendency to go her own way despite popular opinion or administrative rules, that contributed to the multiple failures in communication that occurred before her disappearance.

A Time of Transition

As Amelia grew into a young woman, her mother continued to push for a better life and education for her daughters. The family moved several times, ultimately landing in Chicago, Illinois. Amelia graduated from Hyde Park High School in June 1916. That year, a new educational opportunity arrived in the form of an inheritance. Amelia's mother used the money to enroll Amelia in Ogontz School, a junior college outside of Philadelphia, Pennsylvania. Here Amelia made new friends, some of whom would prove to be valuable connections, and undertook a level of scholarship that challenged her sharp mind and expansive curiosity. She particularly enjoyed classes in art and science.

Amelia at her 1916 graduation from high school

World War I raged during this time, from 1914 to 1918. In 1917, during her winter holiday, Amelia visited her sister Muriel, who was attending school in Toronto in Ontario, Canada. One day, on the streets of Toronto, Amelia saw four soldiers, each missing a leg, walking on crutches down the street. Twenty-year-old Amelia was moved by the sight, and within a week she decided to drop out of school to volunteer as a nurse's aide. As a nurse's aide, Amelia worked herself to near exhaustion, a pattern she would continue for most of her life.

WORKING TO EXHAUSTION: Amelia continued to work herself to near exhaustion for much of her life. After her disappearance, some friends speculated that overwork, illness, and fatigue had made Amelia too tired to do her best and contributed to her untimely end.

In Toronto, Amelia also discovered her love of flying. The hospital where she volunteered was near a military airfield. Pilots invited Amelia and Muriel to see the airplanes. They were not allowed to ride in the planes but instead watched from the field. Amelia returned many times to watch the planes fly and also attended an air show at the Canadian National Exposition Grounds.

Chapter 3

An Adventurer's Life

In 1920, Earhart traveled to Los Angeles, California, where her father was living. On Christmas Day in 1920, Amelia's father took her to the opening of a new airfield in Long Beach, California. The event was marked by an air show, common in aviation at that time, which included air races, aerobatics, and stunts such as wing-walking. Earhart was hooked. Three days later, Earhart took her first ride in an airplane at Rogers Field in Los Angeles, California. Of the experience, she said, "As soon as we left the ground, I knew I myself had to fly."[1]

Not many American women in the 1920s and 1930s worked outside the home, let alone flew as pilots. Earhart was one of the first women to learn how to fly an airplane.

Early Lessons

Earhart first visited Kinner Field in Los Angeles, in January 1921 in search of a flying teacher. Earhart wore a suit and white gloves and had styled her blonde hair in braids wrapped around her head. Anita "Neta" Snook, the field manager, saw a tall, thin woman with an elegant and direct manner approach the airfield with her father.

Neta, one of a few female pilots at the time, had purchased and rebuilt a military airplane. She stored

Earhart with Neta Snook, *left*, her first flight instructor

it at Kinner Field, where she worked on planes and took passengers for rides. Thrilled at the idea of learning to fly from a woman, Earhart signed up for lessons with Neta and immediately took to flying.

Within a year, however, Neta had married her sweetheart and given up flying. By then, Earhart had earned her national flying license and owned her own plane, an Airster given to her by her mother. Going against tradition, she cut her blonde hair short and bought herself a leather jacket, both of which would become part of her trademark look in years to come.

Eager to learn more, Earhart signed up with a new teacher, John G. "Monte" Montijo, one of the best pilots in the area. Monte was impressed with his new student. He let Earhart fly solo after only seven hours of lessons.

A STUDIOUS DAREDEVIL: Earhart showed up at her first flying lesson carrying a library book about aeronautics. She cut a fine figure in a tailored jacket, riding pants, and lace-up boots. During her first lesson, she learned to taxi the plane, and within a month, she had flown the plane a total of four hours.

On October 22, 1922, Earhart completed what would become the first of many record-breaking flights. In a hair-raising flight through fog and sleet, she flew her Airster to 14,000 feet (4,300 m), higher than that type of plane had ever been flown before. Biographer Doris Rich wrote, "She was meticulous in arranging for the [instruments] to prove what she had done but showed far less concern about the capabilities of the plane or her own safety."[2]

In May 1923, Earhart received her international pilot's license from the Fédération Aéronautique Internationale (FAI), or International Aeronautical

Amelia named her first plane the *Canary*. It was a bright yellow Airster with a 28-foot (8.5-m) wingspan.

Federation. She was the sixteenth woman in the world to receive FAI certification.

In 1924, Earhart moved to Boston, Massachusetts, and began a job as social worker. For a time, Earhart still considered flying a "hobby," though it was a busy one.[3] In addition to flying on the weekends, she acted as a sales representative and demonstration flyer on the East Coast and started a women's flying association. By July 1927, Earhart had become a stockholder in one of the nation's first commercial airline companies, Dennison Airport. This time of her life set the course for what would remain two important lifelong interests, a commitment to equal rights—specifically promoting female flyers—and to commercial aviation.

From Student to World-Famous Flyer

To earn the public's enthusiastic attention—and to earn money—an adventurer needed to continue making longer or more fantastic journeys. For flying, this meant taking greater risks by going higher, farther, and faster. In addition, most famous explorers of the early twentieth century wrote books that helped to publicize their adventures, including Admiral Richard Byrd, who made legendary expeditions to the Arctic and the Antarctic, and aviator Charles Lindbergh, who was the first person to fly solo across the Atlantic Ocean. Publicist and publisher George Palmer Putnam helped bring both titles into print, and he had a special skill for making people famous.

In 1928, five years after Earhart broke her first record, she met

Earhart stood out for her elegant clothing and serious manner. As she grew in experience, she continued to develop her unique style, and it played a vital role in her fame. Today, her first leather flying jacket is on display in the National Air and Space Museum in Washington DC.

Putnam was the publicist and promoter for Lindbergh's flight and Byrd's polar expeditions before meeting Earhart.

Putnam and began her journey to fame. It began with a phone call from Captain Hilton Railey, a friend of Putnam, asking if she were willing to do "something for aviation which might be hazardous."[4] Earhart soon discovered that the mysterious request would make her the first woman to fly across the

Atlantic, a dangerous journey that had resulted in the loss of 14 people at sea in the past year, including three women.

The secret venture was funded by wealthy heiress Amy Guest and organized by Putnam. Guest had wanted to make the flight herself, but her family convinced her to find a substitute. Soon Earhart found herself in Putnam's office. The publisher was quickly struck by the aviator's grace and style, as well her resemblance to national aviation hero Charles Lindbergh. Putnam immediately hatched a plan to capitalize on this resemblance and to bring this young female pilot the attention of the world. He even had Earhart mimic the poses Lindbergh had used in publicity photos.

After much planning and organizing, Earhart joined a crew of three to fly across the Atlantic. She would ride as a passenger with the official role of commander, along with pilot Wilmer "Bill" Stultz and copilot and mechanic Louis "Slim" Gordon. They flew a Fokker seaplane with a 72-foot (23-m) wingspan, larger than any Earhart had flown before. It was named the *Friendship*.

After 20 hours and 40 minutes of a difficult 3,000-mile (4,800-km) journey, the *Friendship* landed in Wales on June 18, 1928. Earhart became an instant star and world sensation.

After the flight, Earhart became the focus of both criticism and adoration in the press. Although she generously gave full credit for the flight to the pilot, she received more acclaim than she felt was deserved as a passenger. But any qualms she or the press had about her own ability and bravery as a pilot ended in May 1932, when she made a second flight across the Atlantic. This time she flew by herself and became the first woman to make a solo flight across the Atlantic Ocean.

Over the next ten years, Earhart continued flying, attempting increasingly difficult flights, breaking records, and garnering media attention.

Earhart became the first woman pilot to make the solo trip across the Atlantic Ocean in 1932, flying 2,026 miles (3,260 km) in 14 hours and 56 minutes.

In addition to being the subject of numerous articles, she herself wrote about flying for magazines and newspapers. Her grueling schedule included lectures, photo shoots, and more. Whenever she could, she promoted commercial aviation and equal rights.

Farther and Higher

On July 8, 1933, Earhart broke her own women's speed record for transcontinental flight, flying from Los Angeles to Newark, New Jersey, in 17 hours and 7 minutes. In 1935, she became the first person to fly solo across the Pacific Ocean between California and Hawaii, making the 2,408-mile (3,875-km) journey in 18 hours and 16 minutes. In 1935, she flew 2,100 miles (3,380 km) in 14 hours and 19 minutes, completing the first nonstop flight from Mexico City to Newark.

Her personal and professional life overlapped since most of her time was spent working. After turning down several marriage proposals from Putnam, she finally said yes to her publicist, and the pair wed on February 7, 1931.

Through it all, she made time for flying, attempting increasingly strenuous and heroic flights that earned her international acclaim and attention. The pressure of intense public attention was challenging for Earhart at times, but she undertook it willingly, knowing that it attracted the funds she needed to pursue her dream of flying.

Chapter 4

Around the World

By 1936, Earhart was ready to try for a new and even more elaborate and daring world record: she would be the first woman to fly around the world. It was a risky endeavor. Wiley Post, a close friend of Earhart's, had become the first person to make a solo round-the-world flight in 1933, completing the 15,596-mile (25,099-km) journey in 7 days, 18 hours, and 49 minutes. Since then, other pilots had attempted the trip, but many had died. Earhart's route would be longer than Post's. She would fly closer to the equator, increasing the distance, and she would be the first to cross both the Atlantic and Pacific Oceans, rather than the Arctic Ocean.

Initially, Earhart kept the plan quiet, revealing it only to Putnam. Despite the danger involved, he was enthusiastic about her plan and offered to make all the arrangements for the trip. The first order of business was a new plane. She would need a state-of-the-art aircraft, one more costly than they could afford.

The plane Earhart wanted was a twin-engine Lockheed Electra, which could cruise at a speed of 200 miles per hour

The Electra

Earhart flew a Lockheed Electra on her round-the-world attempt. She first learned about this state-of-the-art twin-engine plane while visiting the Lockheed plant in 1933. Each of the planes built was given a serial number. Earhart's Electra was number 10E and its production began in March 1936.

The plane's wingspan was 55 feet (17 m) and its length was 38 feet 7 inches (11.76 m). Two 550-horsepower Pratt & Whitney S3H-1 engines powered the plane, and it was fitted with constant-speed Hamilton Standard propellers. It also had retractable landing gear and a Sperry Gyropilot, an autopilot device. The exterior of the plane was metal.

Inside, there was a cockpit for the pilot and a small back cabin for the navigator with a table for maps and other navigational instruments. Between the two cabins was a rope on which the pilot and navigator could pass messages to one another because the noise of the propellers made it difficult to hear.

The plane was fitted with six additional fuel tanks, allowing it to hold 1,150 gallons (4,350 l) of gas. The extra fuel doubled the weight of the plane. But adding this kind of extra weight was not uncommon during record-breaking flights.

(320 km/h). It had a price tag of $50,000 and would need an additional $30,000 of equipment to be ready for a world flight, a total of approximately $1.3 million in 2011 dollars.

A Flying Laboratory

One year earlier, Earhart's acclaim—and her steadfast commitment to women's causes and equal rights—had led to an invitation to advise and counsel women

Earhart helped finance her plane by partnering with Purdue University and promising to collaborate on flight research. Today, Purdue holds many of her letters and belongings.

students at Purdue University in West Lafayette, Indiana. Through her connections at the university, and with Putnam's help, she secured funding for the plane.

To avoid attracting attention too early, they called the plane a "flying laboratory" and emphasized that it would be used for aviation research.[1] Putnam hired Paul Mantz, a flight instructor and a friend of Earhart's from California, as the technical adviser to the flight, and Putnam and Mantz began shopping for the plane.

When Mantz made a list of the necessary equipment, Putnam balked at the price. Mantz wanted the best and most modern equipment for the flight, but Putnam, responsible for financing, was concerned about costs. Biographer Doris Rich wrote that Mantz was, "shocked at [Putnam's] attempts to cut costs in bargaining,

Cost versus Safety

Tension between cost and safety plagued Earhart's world flight until its mysterious end. After the plane's loss, many have speculated that cost cutting could have compromised safety. For example, Putnam wanted to paint the plane gold and black, the colors of Purdue University, while Mantz wanted to paint it orange or red for easier location if the plane crashed. In this and many other debates, Earhart won out, and the plane's shimmering aluminum surface remained unpainted.

Earhart discusses aeronautics with a group of young students. To raise money for the pricey Lockheed Electra, Earhart delivered paid lectures across the country.

which suggested to [him] an indifference to Amelia's safety."[2]

A Rocky Start

Meanwhile, Earhart continued her busy schedule. She made a 30-stop lecture tour around the United States followed by 19 additional appearances, delivering a total of 150 lectures in 1936 and earning $45,000. But this was not enough to pay for a flight around the world.

With her biggest and most dangerous flight ahead of her, Earhart was getting tired. She was 39 years old and had endured a grueling schedule for years. She suffered from serious sinus infections and her stomach had never fully adjusted to flying in wildly jostling cabins filled with the smell of fuel. In addition, the pressure of constant promotion had put a strain on her marriage.

A Trial Run

In August 1936, Earhart took her first flight in the Electra. This plane was larger and far more sophisticated than any plane she had flown before. It also had more dials and other instruments in the cockpit, more than 100 in all. To fully master the new machine, Mantz wanted her to fly it more hours than the busy Earhart had time for. She decided to enter the Bendix Trophy Race, a speed competition that went across the United States, in order to gain experience flying her new plane.

She entered the Bendix with friend and fellow aviator Helen Richey as her copilot. Just after takeoff, the navigator's hatch flew dangerously open and had to be tied with a rag. Earhart also had numerous problems with the complicated fuel system; whether this was due to faulty equipment or her lack of knowledge was unclear. Despite these challenges, the Electra finished the race, but barely. The pair came in fifth and last.

Mounting Pressure

Conflicts between Mantz and Putnam continued, and Earhart was pressured from both sides. Mantz

The shiny silver Electra was larger and more complex than any of Earhart's previous planes.

wanted the plane back in California while Putnam
thought it should be at Purdue. Mantz wanted her
to spend more time practicing in the Electra, and
Putnam had arranged more promotional events and
speaking engagements.

Initially, the two men also disagreed over her
choice of navigator. Earhart chose Harry Manning,
who was a skilled navigator at sea but had little
experience in aerial navigation. Putnam wanted to
hire Fred Noonan, a star navigator for Pan American
Airlines, who had made 18 flights across the Pacific
before leaving his job. But whether he had resigned
over differences in pay or was let go for alcoholism
was unclear.

On March 13,
1937, not long
before the flight
was scheduled
to leave, Earhart
decided to take
both navigators
along on the first
leg of her journey.
Noonan would
navigate on the
difficult journey

Exclusive Arrangement

Likely worried about the lack of cash,
Putnam went back on an agreement
he had made with Lockheed to allow
updates on the world flight to be
available to all news outlets. Instead, he
set up an exclusive agreement with the
New York Herald Tribune for Earhart
to write an account of the trip. Though
Putnam was known for aggressive
tactics, this could be seen as an act
of desperation, or at least mounting
anxiety, about the costly flight.

to Howland Island while Manning, a skilled radio operator, would man the radio. After that, Manning would navigate on the next leg of the trip, and then Earhart would complete the rest of her journey alone.

Earhart remained as busy as ever before the flight. She gave speeches in support of President Roosevelt's campaign for reelection and spent time with an old friend, aviator and former head of the Bureau of Air Commerce Gene Vidal, and a new friend, aviator Jacqueline Cochran Oldham.

She also made time for more flight lessons with another teacher, the designer of the Electra, Clarence "Kelly" Johnson. With Johnson as copilot, Earhart practiced flying the plane at different weights, altitudes, and engine settings and learned to use the Cambridge analyzer, an instrument that would allow the plane to use just

Cutting Corners

On March 9, 1936, Robert R. Reining, chief of registration for the Bureau of Air Commerce, notified Earhart that her transport license, or certification to fly, needed to be renewed and that she would have to take an additional instrument-rating exam because her proposed flight included long distances over water. But Earhart interpreted the note in such a way that she only took one portion of the difficult three-part test, skipping the written exam and the radio navigation test.

the right amount of fuel for maximum mileage. Johnson found her to be a good pilot.

Between campaigning, lecturing, and learning to fly the new plane, Earhart received notice from the Bureau of Air Commerce that her flight license would expire mid-trip. She would need to renew it before she could be cleared for takeoff.

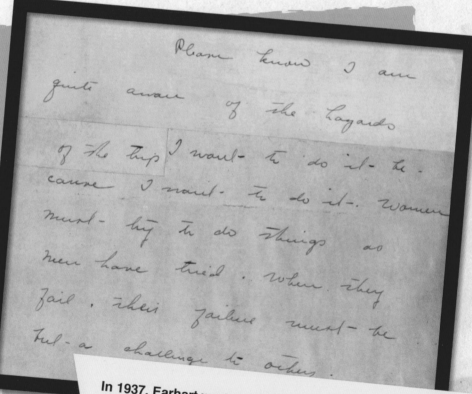

In 1937, Earhart wrote to Putnam, "Women must try to do things as men have tried. When they fail, their failure must be but a challenge to others."

Friends in High Places

Putnam planned the route of the world flight for maximum attention. Earhart would fly from east to west along the equator. But in order to fly over international waters and to land on foreign soil, it was necessary to arrange agreements between the United States and other governments. Putnam wrote many letters on behalf of Earhart in an effort to clear these diplomatic hurdles, but it was getting more difficult for an individual adventurer to get government assistance.

The world had changed since Earhart started flying. An economic depression hit the United States and spread to the international community. People were more interested in politics and the economy than flights of fancy made by explorers.

But Earhart was in luck; until just a month before her departure, her good friend Gene Vidal was chief of the Bureau of Air Commerce, and he helped facilitate many of the arrangements for her flight. In addition, she had been close with Eleanor Roosevelt, the First Lady, since her flight on the *Friendship*.

When Putnam failed to get anywhere with the navy in requesting assistance for the world flight, in particular in building the landing strip at Howland Island, Earhart wrote a letter to the president himself, ending with the lines, "Knowing your own enthusiasm for voyaging and your affectionate interest in Navy matters, I am asking you to help me secure Navy cooperation—that is, if you think well of the project."[3]

Within a week, the chief of Naval Operations received notice that, "the President hoped the navy would do what they could to cooperate with Miss Amelia Earhart in her proposed flight."[4] The note was effective; both the navy and the Coast Guard went to great effort and expense to build a runway and support the flight.

MILITARY AID: Military records suggest that some soldiers in the navy and the Coast Guard resented the expense, time, and effort the military devoted to supporting the flight of a single civilian in an effort to fly around the world, a feat that had already been accomplished.

Chapter 5

The Final Journey

In March 1937, Earhart was preparing to take off for Honolulu, Hawaii, and begin her round-the-world journey. The plane was ready to go when navigator Noonan discovered that it lacked an important navigational instrument. Despite elaborate preparations, the only navigational instrument aboard was an ordinary sextant, used to navigate ships. He wanted a modern bubble octant, an expensive instrument used at the time in commercial aircraft and one he had used when working for commercial airline Pan Am. Manning, a former navy man, wired a naval air station in San Diego, California, requesting to borrow one. The modern bubble octant was sent to Oakland, California, where the plane was waiting, and they took off for Hawaii on March 17.

Perhaps exhausted from all the preparations, or maybe due to uncertainty with the new plane, Earhart flew only part of the way and requested that Mantz land the plane in Hawaii. Manning, who was on board as one of two navigators, later explained that a brief moment of confusion had ensued when Earhart seemed not to know what was going on. "*That*," Mantz had told her then, "was pilot fatigue."[1]

Away We Go, and Go Again

In the dawn hours of March 20, while attempting to take off from Hawaii, Earhart's journey around the world ended abruptly in a crash on the runway. Initially, Earhart blamed the crash on a wet spot on the runway, but she later changed her statement, saying instead that the left tire blew out.

PILOT FATIGUE: Pilot fatigue offers a possible explanation for what might have happened to Earhart on the final leg of her journey. In the last days of the trip, it is likely she was exhausted and perhaps ill. This could have led to confusion and a possible crash.

The cause of the crash remains unclear, but Earhart had avoided a fiery accident by prudently

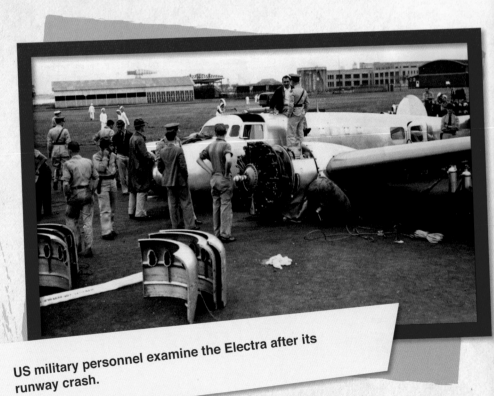

US military personnel examine the Electra after its runway crash.

shutting off the fuel once the plane went off course. An Air Force brigadier general on site praised her bravery and cool nerves.

Others were more critical. Mantz, watching from the ground, felt certain she had done exactly what he had advised against, overcompensating on the throttle until the plane went off course. The US Army Air Corps officer in charge that day was also critical, saying she did not listen to the advice of experts. But he did not say whose advice she had ignored, and his response seemed to be rooted in

Clues from the Runway Crash

The crash on the runway during Earhart's first attempt to fly around the world provides some clues to what might have led to her disappearance. If the plane malfunctioned, as it had during the Bendix Race, it could have had a faulty fuel system or some other mechanical problem that became an issue during the final flight.

If, as Mantz suggested, she was not yet skilled enough to fly the plane, it is possible that lingering uncertainty with the plane's instruments led to a final crash. The opinion of the officer in charge, that she ignored the advice of experts, is questionable because he failed to say who had advised her. But his opinion is important because this attitude foreshadowed a growing disconnect between Earhart's approach and military protocol. She was an adventurer and a woman. To many in the all-male military, which supported the flight only because the president commanded it, the Earhart journey was a dangerous stunt and a drain on precious time and resources.

what he perceived as her disrespectful attitude toward the military.

A disappointed Earhart sailed back to the mainland. She spent the next few months with friends, resting and recuperating from exhaustion. The Electra was shipped to Lockheed, where it underwent significant repairs.

Loving Husband and Busy Promoter

Putnam's aggressive publicity tactics were well known to all, and many claimed he pressured Earhart to attempt the world trip. But his personal correspondence revealed otherwise. After the crash on the runway in Honolulu, Putnam wrote to her of the flight and its hazards: "I love you dearly—and I don't want you to run risks."[2]

The crash posed new problems for the flight. It reminded all involved of how dangerous the journey was and perhaps unnerved the pilot and her crew.

While the plane was being repaired, Earhart and Putnam addressed changes in the flight. Due to concerns about storms expected late in the flight, Earhart decided to change directions and fly from west to east around the equator this time. This would mean trying to spot tiny Howland Island in the sea at the end of the long journey.

There was also a change in personnel. Manning left the crew, leaving Noonan as the sole navigator. At the time, Manning blamed it on work, but he later said, "I got very fed up with her bull-headedness several times."[3] This characterization is plausible, given Earhart's history of going her own way, but Manning could also have felt slighted at her decision to include a second navigator.

The loss of Manning had important consequences. It left Earhart with a navigator who had a reputation for alcoholism. Making matters worse, Noonan had recently been involved in a two-car collision that caused Earhart to question his promise to stay away from alcohol. But he was a

Who Was Unfit?

Earhart reported "personnel unfitness," on the last leg of her journey, but whether she referred to her own exhaustion or Noonan's drinking has never been clarified. In an exhaustive examination of records related to the final flight, Ric Gillespie, founder and director of the International Group for Historic Aircraft Recovery (TIGHAR), wrote, "Fred Noonan's professional record, both nautical and aeronautical, is spotless."[4] But others speculate that Noonan was an alcoholic and had been drinking before the final flight.

good navigator; finding the tiny landing strip on Howland Island was going to be a challenge, and by now both Putnam and Mantz felt Noonan was the man for the job. Perhaps the more pressing issue was that Manning had been the only person in the crew skilled at using Morse code.

Since neither she nor Noonan could use Morse code, Earhart decided to have the wire needed to use it taken off the plane. Without Morse code as an option, the only means of communication with land would be voice transmission by radio. However, Earhart had skipped the radio portion of the Instrument Training exam.

While the plane was at Lockheed being repaired, Putnam hired radioman

Morse Code

Earhart's primary communication system for her flight was voice, or spoken radio. However, at the time, many ships and airplanes also used Morse code, an older system used to send telegraph messages. Morse code translates the alphabet into a series of dots and dashes. These are typed into a transmitter and sent through the air. Morse code was an important backup system that could be heard at greater distances than voice radio messages. Morse code might have allowed Earhart to maintain contact with the Howland Island crew. To use Morse code, it was necessary to know the code and to carry a transmitting wire, called a trailing wire, under the plane. However, neither Earhart nor Noonan were skilled in Morse code.

Joseph Gurr to repair and test the radio. He reinstalled the antennae, moving them forward on the plane to help improve the range and capacity of the radio.

The radio receiver aboard the plane had a direction finder loop, which was capable of locating the direction of a radio range station. Using this device, the pilot could adjust the antenna from inside the cockpit, tuning the radio. This was vital because messages had to be in the same range when sent and received in order to be heard.

Earhart took the Electra for a test flight around San Francisco Bay before setting out on her around-the-world flight.

When Gurr offered to review the use of the
direction finder loop with Earhart, it was apparent
to him she did not know how to operate it. She
had used it only once before, when flying to
Honolulu with Manning on board. He gave her a
training session, but it was cut short due to her busy
schedule. In addition, the loop was not working well,
and no one had time to investigate the problem.

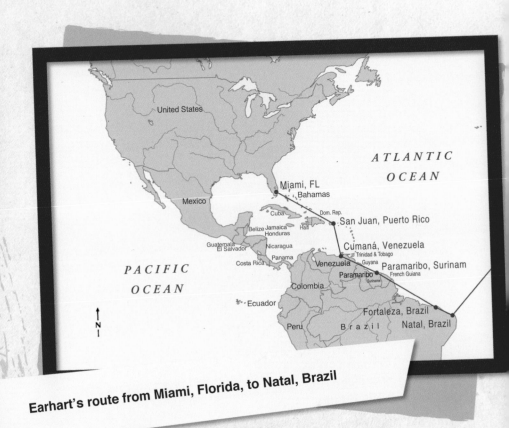

Earhart's route from Miami, Florida, to Natal, Brazil

A Great Adventure

At 5:56 a.m. on June 1, 1937, Earhart set off from Miami, Florida, in the Electra along with Noonan as navigator. They flew along the eastern coast of Central and South America for six days, stopping in Puerto Rico, Venezuela, Surinam, and Brazil. Most nights, Earhart slept approximately five hours, waking before the sun rose. Earhart let the Sperry automatic pilot fly much of the way as she took notes for newspaper articles and for a book commissioned about the flight.

From there, they flew across the Atlantic, headed for Dakar in Africa. They hit bad weather on the way. In a note sent to a friend, Noonan wrote that the flight had "produced the worst weather we have experienced—heavy rain and dense cloud formations necessitated blind flying for ten of the thirteen hours we were in flight."[5] During the 13 hour and 22 minute journey, the weather prohibited Noonan

> ONE MORE FLIGHT: "I have a feeling there is just one more flight in my system," Earhart told a friend before setting off on her final journey. "This trip around the world is it."[6]

from using his navigational instruments for much of the time.

As they approached Africa, Noonan was finally able to get an accurate reading on their location. From his seat in the back of the plane, gazing at charts spread out on the table, he sent Earhart notes guiding her to correct their position so they would land in Dakar, in what is today Senegal but was then part of French West Africa. Instead, they landed 163 miles (262 km) north in the city of Saint-Louis, also in Senegal. The reason for the error is unclear; in her articles, Earhart said it was her fault. But it is also possible that she took the blame for a navigational error, hoping to persuade officials not to fine or stop the plane for landing somewhere other than what was arranged with the local governments.

RADIO TROUBLES: In a letter to a friend about the stormy flight from South America to Africa, Noonan wrote, "And our radio was out of order—it would be in such a jam."[7] This indicates the crew was already having trouble with the radio. Whether this was due to the weather (as Noonan surmised), lack of knowledge, or malfunction was unclear.

At this point, Earhart had flown more than 40 hours, covering 4,000 miles (6,400 km). The next day, June 8, the Electra made the short flight to

Dakar, where the plane was held up for two days due
to bad weather. On June 10, likely impatient to be
on her way, Earhart changed their next destination,
and they flew to Gao in modern-day Mali,
successfully flying 1,140 miles (1,830 km) between a
sandstorm to the north and a tornado to the south.
The next day, they continued on, flying in searing
heat over the Sahara Desert to arrive in Chad. A day
later, they flew 1,200 miles (1,930 km) to the Red
Sea in modern-day Eritrea.

Earhart's route from Natal, Brazil, to Karachi, Pakistan

On June 15, Earhart flew the Electra nearly 2,000 miles (3,200 km) across the Red Sea, landing in Karachi in what is Pakistan today after 13 hours and 20 minutes. Along the way, the fuel analyzer, which allowed her maximum fuel use, broke. It would not be repaired for several days until they arrived in Indonesia where the Dutch airline KLM had mechanics who could work on the plane.

Earhart and Noonan spent two days in Pakistan. Earhart went on two camel rides. On June 17, they set out again, flying across the continent to Calcutta in India, which was under British control at the time. It was an exceedingly hot and difficult journey. Rainstorms and shifting currents tossed the Electra as much as 1,000 feet (305 m) up or down within seconds, but they arrived safely.

Taking off from a waterlogged runway, the Electra crossed the Bay of Bengal. The plane headed to Akyab, Burma, where Earhart and Noonan stopped to refuel. They flew through 400 miles (640 km) of monsoon rains to reach Rangoon, Burma, where they landed on June 19. They spent the brief stopover as guests of the US consul and visited the Golden Pagoda.

They set out for Bangkok in Thailand, called Siam at the time, where they refueled before flying to Singapore's new multimillion dollar airport. From there, they flew to Bandung, Indonesia, then called Java and part of the Netherlands, where the plane would get an overhaul by KLM mechanics. Before landing in Bandung, Earhart "circled the field for fifteen minutes on a clear day, apparently unable to see the airdrome markers."[8]

Earhart had flown a total of 20,000 miles (32,200 km) in 135 hours over 21 days. She had

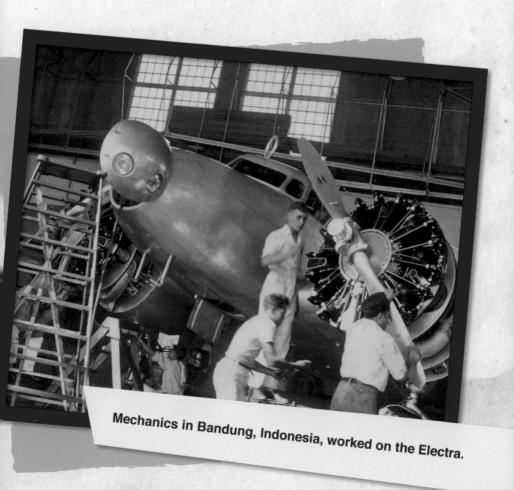

Mechanics in Bandung, Indonesia, worked on the Electra.

slept little and reportedly suffered from diarrhea and nausea throughout the trip. She and Noonan remained in Bandung for six days while KLM mechanics, familiar with the Electra and its instruments, worked on the plane. Earhart and Noonan stayed with friends of Noonan's in Jakarta, Indonesia's capital, which was called Batavia at the time. At one point, they started out again, but were

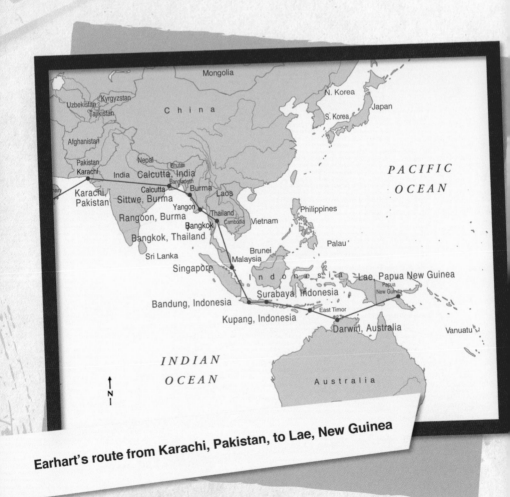

Earhart's route from Karachi, Pakistan, to Lae, New Guinea

forced to return after a quick flight for more work on the Electra.

It was not until June 27 that the plane was pronounced ready and its instruments, including the Cambridge fuel analyzer, corrected. Earhart and Noonan set off on the next leg of the journey. They made a five-hour flight to the island of Timor then flew on to Port Darwin, Australia, where they landed on June 28.

While in Darwin, the head of the airport's radio direction-finding unit pulled Earhart aside to ask why she had not used her radio upon approach to Darwin. It was mandatory to do so upon arrival. She explained that she had had problems with the radio since setting out. He investigated, repaired a blown fuse, and provided her with additional fuses to use should she need them.

They made the 1,200-mile (1,930-km) trip to Lae, New Guinea, on June 29. Despite bad weather, radio problems, and stops for repairs, they had traveled a total of 22,000 miles (35,400 km) over almost 40 days. Earhart was exhausted. In a call to Putnam, she mentioned "personnel unfitness," but whether she worried for herself or her navigator was unclear.[9] Their longest and most difficult trip, the approach to Howland Island, lay ahead.

Chapter 6

Searching for Earhart

On June 30, Earhart wrote in her post to the *Herald Tribune*, "Lockheed [Electra] stands ready for longest hop weighted with gasoline and oil to capacity."[1] The plane was loaded with more than 1,100 gallons (4,160 l) to make the 2,556-mile (4,113-km) flight.

It was necessary to calculate the fuel accurately to make their destination. The Cambridge fuel analyzer had been repaired in Indonesia, but it was still relatively unfamiliar to Earhart, and it had malfunctioned more than once. In addition, the radio had been causing problems all along. Not only was it necessary for communication, but it was also needed to accurately set the time on Noonan's chronometer, a time-keeping instrument used in navigation. But it appeared that everything had been repaired.

In order to carry the amount of fuel necessary, Earhart and Noonan had to strip away nearly everything for this last leg of the journey. Tossed aside were flares, smoke bombs, some tools and spare parts, and some survival equipment. How much and what was left behind remains unknown.

They took off at approximately 10:00 a.m. that morning, local time, but not before Henry Balfour, the New Guinea Airways radio operator at Lae, assisted Earhart with her radio, which was malfunctioning again. As soon as the silver plane lifted off the runway and winged into the air, Balfour sent a priority message to the *Itasca*, the

Ready for Anything?

The type and amount of survival gear Earhart and Noonan carried would have directly affected their ability to survive in the sea or on land if the plane went down. Putnam notified rescuers that the plane had life vests, a rubber raft, and a pistol on board, but this might have been wishful thinking. According to Earhart scholar Gillespie, "No one on the United States, including Putnam, could possibly have known what emergency gear was aboard the aircraft on the Lae-Howland flight."[2]

US Coast Guard ship waiting off Howland Island and tasked with supporting the flight, to inform them of the Electra's takeoff time and its expected arrival in 18 hours.

Confusion on the Ground

For seven hours, Balfour remained in touch with Earhart via radio. Many of these transmissions were marred by static and difficult to hear. And though he sent her the most recent weather forecast, she did not acknowledge receipt of the message, likely indicating she did not receive it. The clearest of Earhart's messages were sent at a frequency of 6210 kilohertz, and Balfour suggested she stay tuned to that frequency. Late that afternoon, Balfour received a message with her position. She was on course and 750 miles (1,200 km) out. It was the only time in the flight that she could be heard to report her position, and it was the last message Balfour received from her.

Off shore of Howland, the *Itasca* waited for a signal from the plane. A series of miscommunications and lost messages led to a very confusing situation.

Three people were responsible for coordinating the flight to Howland Island: Putnam, Commander Warner K. Thompson, and Richard B. Black, the government administrator who had successfully coordinated the construction of the new runways on Howland. As the Electra made its way to the small island, all three were involved in communicating information about weather, arrival times, and the plane's radio capabilities.

In the midst of all this, Bellarts's radio operators aboard the *Itasca* had not received

Frequency Errors

Earhart planned to send messages at 3105 and 6210 kilohertz and requested to be contacted by voice on these two frequencies. She also requested that the *Itasca* send her a series of letter *A*s on 7500 kilohertz as she approached to help her hone in on the signal and find the island. But the ship had only one high frequency transmitter to do both of these operations, so they had to switch off doing one and then the other.

Of Earhart's messages, only those sent at 3105 were received clearly by the *Itasca*. The radiomen aboard the *Itasca* tried to contact her as requested on 3105 and to send a series of *A*s on 7500 kilohertz when she approached. In an effort to reach her, they also tried other signals. But many of the messages they sent Earhart would have been outside the range of her radio's capacity.

the message that neither Earhart nor Noonan could use Morse code. Along with radio transmissions, they continued to send messages in Morse code for several hours—to no avail. Making matters worse, the radio signal Earhart would use had not been clearly communicated to the ship. Commander Thompson himself had sent several messages to Putnam and

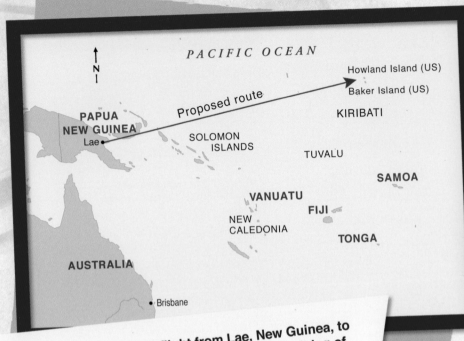

The 2,556-mile (4,113-km) flight from Lae, New Guinea, to Howland Island was the longest and most difficult leg of Earhart's route.

Earhart to discover the radio signal but had received conflicting reports about the transmission signal and the radio's capabilities.

Time, too, posed a problem. Earhart had clearly stated when she would send messages. But the navy and the Coast Guard were accustomed to operating on half hour time zones while at sea, so while she sent her messages at the scheduled times, clocks aboard the ship read 30 minutes earlier. As a result, the radiomen mistakenly believed she was willfully going against her plan and formed the impression that she was a lone flyer who did as she pleased.

Despite this impression, Bellarts and his radio crew continued to listen attentively to what they understood to be the correct signal and to send messages at what they thought were the agreed upon times. In an effort to reach her one way or another, they also sent Morse code signals, listened to radio ranges beyond what they had been told she would use, and tried sending messages on a variety of signals. Despite their best efforts, no one heard from Earhart until Bellarts received the 2:45 a.m. message.

A flurry of inconsistent and mostly unclear messages followed. But without the correct signal, the voice messages could not be heard or received. Nineteen hours into the flight, the radio room finally heard a message from the plane that was loud and clear. The radio

No Signal

The ship had a low-frequency direction-finder. Only the Morse code antenna could have picked up the direction-finder's signals, but the antenna had been removed from the plane. Thus, the ship could not track Earhart's signals. There was a high-frequency direction-finder on Howland Island that could have tuned into Earhart's signals, but it used so much battery power that it was depleted after listening for the plane all night. It was unusable on the next critical day as the Electra approached.

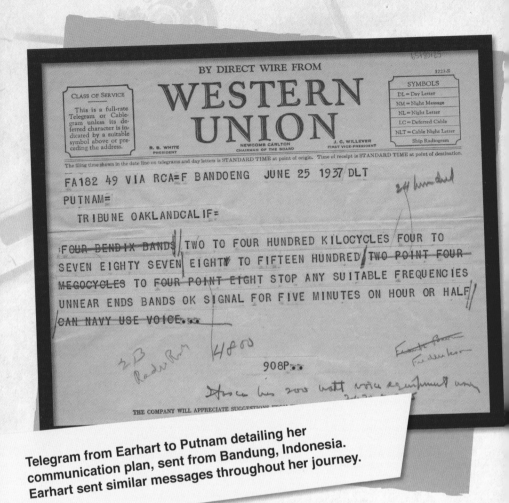

Telegram from Earhart to Putnam detailing her communication plan, sent from Bandung, Indonesia. Earhart sent similar messages throughout her journey.

operator that logged the call wrote that she had said, "We must be on you but cannot see you, but gas is running low. Have been unable to reach you by radio. We are flying at 1,000 feet [305 m]."[3] She was reportedly overhead, but there was no sign of a plane anywhere above the ship. It seemed clear she was lost at sea.

Searching the Pacific

Captain Thompson abandoned the *Itasca*'s stationary position offshore and began searching the sea. He tried to piece together bits of information from the many short and incomplete messages

HOPING AGAINST HOPE: Howland Island resident James Kamakaiwi was the namesake of the airstrip that lay waiting for the Earhart plane. He expressed the sentiments of many involved, saying, "I couldn't make myself believe Amelia had missed us. We kept watching the sky. The *Itasca* started out to sea towards the northwest. Soon she was disappearing over the horizon. I hope with all my heart they find her."[5]

received from the Earhart plane and deduced that she had "passed to the north and west" of Howland, run out of fuel, and gone down in the sea "within 100 miles [160 km]" northwest of Howland.[4] None of this information had been made completely clear from the reports received, but as the commander in charge, he surely felt responsible to take action as time was running short. He set the ship out on a comprehensive search of the sea that would last for several days.

Commander Thompson sent an "all ships" alert, requesting vessels to listen for any distress or other calls from the plane: "Possibility plane may use radio on either 3105, 6210, or 500 [kilohertz] voice.

Request any vessel [in] that vicinity listen for calls and contact *Itasca*."[6] The local Pan Am airline radio station at Mokapu Point near Honolulu also began to tune in on three signals to listen for the plane.

Cries of Distress

As the *Itasca* carefully searched the ocean, the men in the radio room continued to send signals on many frequencies with little success. Listening at all hours, they received intermittent signals and broken messages indicating that Earhart was still alive and trying to connect with the ship. The tension and stress in her voice was clearly mounting. The messages were either too short or on the wrong signal for the ship to get a bearing and locate the direction.

Growing frustrated, they continued to man the radios and keep a running log of all communications.

Putnam anxiously awaited news in California, trying to gather as much information as

CALLING *ITASCA*: Radio operators use a code name to identify themselves. The Electra's code was KHAQQ. Operators across the Pacific listened attentively, waiting to hear "KHAQQ calling Itasca."[7]

he could and communicate it to the search. At the same time, callers from various spots in the United

States began to report hearing Earhart's radio transmissions. Some of these were soon revealed to be fakes. Others contained personal information that suggested they could have come from Earhart, although many experts contend the signals could not have been heard so far away.

Log Discrepancies

Radio operators had to write down a lot of information quickly. Also, the different operators on duty might not have heard things exactly the same way. Because of this, the logs often had errors and revisions. It was common practice to clean and retype these for the official record. Knowing the importance of the Earhart trip, chief radio operator Bellarts saved his original radio log so it could be compared with the official log later.

One of the people to reportedly hear Earhart's calls was Betty Klenck in Florida. Tuning the family radio to find a program, she paused to hear a woman say, "This is Amelia Earhart. This is Amelia Earhart."[8] Not knowing what to do, the teenager wrote down everything she heard over the next few hours. Her notebook relays a distressing story filled with bits of conversation between a man and a woman. It was clear they were lost and in need of help. The man was hurt and at one point said, "Help, help, I need air."[9]

From the conversation, Betty thought the plane had crashed on land but was filling with water. This fit in with reports from other amateur radio operators in Texas and Wyoming who said they heard Earhart and understood her to be on a reef. The listener in Texas thought the plane was "partially on land, part in water."[10]

This information could have been helpful to the rescuers but either did not reach them in time or was not considered important since it came from amateurs. The confusion and pressure to find Earhart and Noonan before it was too late had led to a tense and dramatic situation. On July 3, newspapers around the world began to report that the famous flyer and her navigator had gone missing.

The Suitcase

Listening to what she believed to be Earhart on her home radio in Florida, the teenage Betty Klenck heard the distressed woman say, "George, get the suitcase in my closet . . . California."[11] This seemingly mundane sentence provides an intimate clue that Betty really could have been listening to the real Earhart. Four years earlier, in a letter to her mother, Earhart had asked that, should anything ever happen to her, the suitcase of private papers stored in her closet in California be destroyed.

Transfer of Power

Over the next few days, the hope that Earhart and Noonan would be found alive diminished. The military had already gone to great expense. After day five, with no sign of the plane, the navy took control of the rescue attempt from the Coast Guard. Admiral Murfin, the man placed at the head of the navy search team, limited the search to seven more days.

The navy battleship *Colorado* was steaming toward Howland and ready to begin searching,

Seaplanes similar to this Catalina model searched in vain for Earhart.

as was the navy ship *Swan*, stationed between Howland and Honolulu. A seaplane was also sent but had to turn back due to bad weather and a risky landing. The *Lexington,* an aircraft carrier with three destroyers and 67 small scouting planes, headed from California to Howland Island.

Following up on the possibility that the plane had gone down on a reef, the two ships searched the sea and the area around a small group of islands near Howland, the Phoenix and Gilbert Islands, but turned up empty-handed. When the aircraft carrier arrived, small planes roared off its deck and into the clear sky over the Pacific to make an additional overhead search of each of the islands in the area. But they too came back with nothing of note to report.

President Roosevelt had spared no expense in searching for the missing heroine. Reporters that criticized this expense, protesting that the government spent $4 million, received an earful when the president retorted that, "any citizen, rich or poor, would receive this sort of help."[12] But no rescue mission this large had ever been launched for a single US citizen. Four thousand men had searched an area of 25,000 square miles (64,750 sq km). The 16-day search was called off on July 19, 1937.

At the conclusion of the official search, Putnam launched an additional search of several islands in the vicinity, including the Phoenix and Gilbert Islands, but this search, too, concluded with no trace of the Electra.

Today, researchers use sonar equipment to explore the deep ocean in hopes of finding Earhart's plane.

Chapter 7

Theories and Possibilities

During the 1920s and 1930s, flying was a dangerous business. Many world-class aviators, as well as quite a few lesser-known flyers, went down with their planes. Accidents, even fatal ones, were not uncommon. Earhart certainly knew this. From her first flight across the Atlantic aboard the *Friendship*, she had prepared for the worst, writing letters to family members to say her good-byes and taking care of financial business. As her career progressed, the fearless flyer had said, "When I go, I would like to go in my plane. Quickly."[1]

The mystery of her disappearance has left questions about whether she got her wish.

Did she go down quickly with her plane? Or were she and Noonan stranded on an island in the Pacific for days? If they went down at sea, did they have access to a raft so they could float while awaiting possible rescuers? None of these questions have clear or certain answers. What happened during Earhart's final hours in the air, or in the days afterward while the US government conducted the largest rescue mission in history searching for her, is unknown.

FRIENDS UNITE: As the official search came to an end, a group of Earhart's friends and colleagues started the nonprofit Amelia Earhart Foundation. With Eleanor Roosevelt as honorary chairperson, they aimed to discover what had happened to the missing aviator and navigator. But despite their efforts to raise funds for continued research, no extensive private search was ever conducted.

Mass Confusion

One of the most plausible explanations for what happened can be found in the communication surrounding the final flight. There was no single person in charge of logistics. Instead, many interested parties—Putnam, Mantz, Commander Thompson, and Richard Black primary among them—were trying to get vital information about fuel, flight times, weather, radio capabilities, and more to the people who needed it. Once the rescue began, the chorus of voices grew even louder, with scores of amateur radio operators weighing in. Despite everyone's best intentions, miscommunication was rampant.

In addition to the many voices, communications equipment was much slower than it is today. The Coast Guard and the navy had the most up-to-date equipment, but even they did not have anywhere

Paul Mantz, Earhart's technical adviser, assisted in the rescue effort.

near the level of communications capability that
an average person has now; there was no Internet,
e-mail, cell phones, or satellites. Messages containing
important flight information were sent via telegraph,
a system of sending shorthand messages over wires
and electric currents.

On top of everything else, those
communications took place over multiple time
zones, and some participants were operating on
military time and others on civilian time. One
example of many communication problems was
that the most current weather report from Lae
to Howland, pivotal information for pilot and
navigator, did not arrive in Indonesia until after
Earhart and Noonan were airborne.

Another example of communication failure is
that no one knew exactly how fast or high the Electra
was flying, critical information for determining
how long its fuel would last. Accounts from the Lae
airport indicate the plane carried approximately
1,100 gallons (4,160 l) of gas before it set off for
Howland. It is estimated that in good weather
without wind the Electra could fly between 24 to
27 hours at speeds of between 135 and 150 miles
per hour (217 and 241 km/h). Since reports of
the Electra's speed and the flight's wind conditions

either went unheard or were simply not given, it is impossible to determine exactly when the plane's fuel would have run out.

As Earhart scholar Gillespie explained,

Incomplete information and misconceptions about the flight and its capabilities had crippled Itasca's attempts to guide the flight to a safe landing. Now these misconceptions, compounded by assumptions and bad information, were making it impossible to accurately assess the clues the search had turned up so far.[2]

Earhart's plane was refueled in Darwin, Australia, the last stop before Lae, New Guinea. The plane likely ran out of gas, but no one knows where.

Radio Problems

One probable key to what went wrong lay in the radio. Firstly, there was much confusion about which signal Earhart would be using. In her biography of Earhart, Kathleen Winters noted that, while the Electra was en route to Howland, Commander Thompson "was still trying to nail down the Electra's frequencies and radio schedule."[3] Lack of this key information severely limited communication.

In addition, the airwaves were clogged with reporters and others seeking the latest news about the disappearance. This caused such a problem that in the early hours of the rescue attempt Commander Thompson ordered all communication with the outside world cut off so the radio could be used exclusively for the flight. In addition, many of the radiomen did not know Noonan was onboard, so they disregarded any communication with a male voice. It is easily possible a key transmission was lost in the hubbub.

Even with perfect conditions for transmission, with open airwaves and a clear understanding of frequencies, Earhart had an apparent lack of understanding about how to use her radio for communication and direction finding. She had not spent enough time learning to use it and did

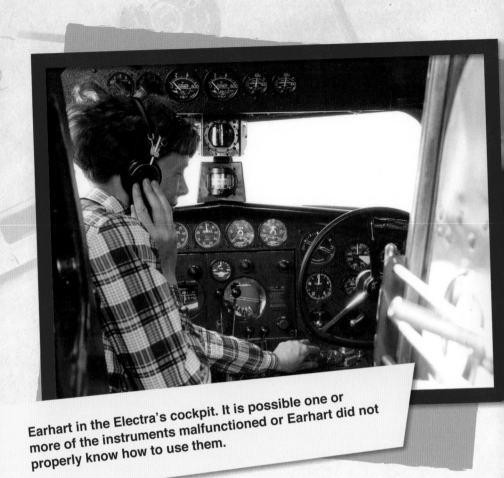

Earhart in the Electra's cockpit. It is possible one or more of the instruments malfunctioned or Earhart did not properly know how to use them.

not seem to recognize its pivotal role in locating Howland Island. Had she thought she was using one frequency when she was really using another? Did she lack the knowledge to use her direction finder?

Perhaps the most important clue to the radio mishaps can be seen in film footage of the Electra's takeoff from Lae. The antenna on the belly, the main antenna for receiving radio transmissions, appears to have been ripped off. Gillespie observed, "As the Electra comes back past the camera on its takeoff run, both motion picture and still photography show that the belly antenna is now missing."[4] If it were really gone, Earhart would not have heard a thing when she attempted to use the primary antenna during the flight.

Conflicting Voices

Another possible key to the confusion surrounding the flight and rescue attempt were the differing perspectives of Earhart and the military tasked with supporting her flight. The Coast Guard and the navy did all they could to accomplish their mission but lacked an understanding of the pilot and her capabilities. Likewise, if Earhart had sent more complete and detailed information, as the military was accustomed to receiving, she could have better helped them assist her.

Given the times, Earhart's background as an outspoken pacifist and as a widely recognized supporter of women's and equal rights could also have influenced

MILITARY OPINION: A log by one of the officers aboard the *Itasca* reflects what seems to have been the prevailing opinion of the military, "We all admired her nerve and pluck to attempt such a flight, but we cannot admire her good sense and judgment in the conduct of it."[5]

the opinion of the military, causing some of them to reach the conclusion that she did not know what she was doing despite evidence to the contrary. With more faith in her abilities, could they have found a solution to the radio problems?

Down at Sea

While the fates of Earhart and Noonan remain unknown, many subsequent researchers have followed Commander Thompson's line of thinking that the Electra ran out of gas and plunged into the sea around Howland Island. The most famous

Elgen Long

Elgen Long was born in 1927 in Oregon. As a nine-year-old boy delivering newspapers, Long read headlines about the Earhart disappearance. These memories became the basis for a lifelong fascination.

Long joined the navy during World War II (1939–1945). He was interested in planes and worked his way up from radio operator to navigator to pilot. At the close of the war in 1945, Long proved his bravery on a particularly risky mission: he and fellow US pilots were tasked with flying over Japanese territory to ensure that the cease-fire would be honored—if it were not, they would have been shot down.

In 1971, Long flew around the world solo, becoming the first person to do so by passing over the North and South Poles. After the flight, he and his wife, Marie, began interviewing anyone they could find who was involved in the Earhart flight. They wrote *Amelia Earhart: The Mystery Solved*, published by Simon & Schuster in 1999. The book details what the Longs believe to have happened on the Electra's final flight—that the airplane crashed into the ocean.

of these theorists is aviator, navigator, adventurer, and author Elgen Long. Based on years of research, Long reconstructed what he believed to have happened to the Electra, concluding that it ran out of gas and sank in the Pacific. He published his findings in 1999.

The first search of the ocean since the *Itasca* scoured the area in 1937 was initiated by Dana Timmer in 1994. Timmer hired deep-sea technology firm Williamson & Associates to conduct an ocean

Nauticos used its own sonar system to search for Earhart in 2002 and 2006.

FAST FLYOVERS: Why did the commander declare the search complete after flying over each island only once? Had the pilots, flying high to avoid local birds and peering at the islands at high tide, missed their chance to spot the downed aviator and navigator?

search. However, the ship Timmer rented was unable to support the cutting-edge technology needed for the search. Five years later, Timmer and a business associate hired Williamson once again. They completed their planned search but did not find the plane.

Additional searches of the sea around Howland Island have been conducted by Nauticos, an underwater exploration company founded by David Jourdan. In 2002, Long joined Nauticos in conducting a search using a deep-sea sonar system the company had designed. They covered 600 square miles (1,550 sq km) of ocean before stopping the search due to equipment issues. A second search, estimated to cost $1.5 million, was scheduled to take place in 2004. But instead, Jourdan and Long teamed up with a nonprofit research organization, the Waitt Institute, in 2006. Together, they assembled a team of experts and made a comprehensive deep-sea search of the area around Howland using a grid method with sonar imaging systems to map the area. Waitt followed up with further surveys in 2009. But again, no evidence of the airplane was discovered.

Alone on an Island

Other theorists believe the Electra went down on a reef that, when the tide came up, would be covered in water. This theory came largely from messages picked up by amateur radios.

Many of the small islands in the Pacific near Howland had reefs, but only the reefs on some uninhabited islands in the Phoenix group were believed to be smooth enough to permit a landing at low tide. At high tide, those same smooth reefs would be covered in water. At the time the Electra would likely have landed or crashed, the tide was out in the Phoenix Islands, so the reefs would have been dry.

With this in mind, the navy sent more than 60 small planes to search the Phoenix and Gilbert Islands. The planes spent an average of five to ten minutes

PSYCHIC ASSISTANCE: Growing increasingly anxious, Putnam followed up on advice that he is thought to have received from a psychic. He sent additional letters and requests to the government seeking increased searches of the area around the Gilbert Islands in the belief that she would be found there. But the navy was simultaneously concluding its search of those islands.

flying over each island. Common sense would indicate this was not enough time to spot signs of life on the islands from above. A contemporary analysis from Civil Air Patrol Probability of Detection concurs, stating that, by 1937 standards, the planes had only a 10 to 20 percent chance of finding the Electra in one flyover. Yet when the last plane returned from its island flyover, the navy declared the search of the Phoenix and Gilbert Islands complete and the rescue attempt ended. Putnam

Signs of Life

Senior Aviator Lieutenant John Lambrecht was at the controls of one of the small planes that roared off the deck of the *Colorado* on the morning of July 9, 1937. The plane took off over the Pacific to search islands in the Phoenix group. The plane flew at an altitude of approximately 400 feet (120 m), and it was unlikely the pilot or crew could accurately estimate the size and scale of anything they saw on the island.

Writing to fellow aviators, though not an official report, Lambrecht described the second island they flew over, Gardner, approximately 350 miles (560 km) south of Howland, this way: "Most of this island is covered with tropical vegetation with, here and there, a grove of coconut palms."[6] He went on, "Here signs of recent habitation were clearly visible, but repeated circling and zooming failed to elicit any answering wave from possible inhabitants, and it was finally taken for granted that none were there."[7]

But if these "signs of life" had any connection to Earhart and Noonan, the navy did not discover it. The pilots did not return to reinvestigate the Gardner Island further, and this seemingly key information was not included in the official record.

organized a search of the islands later that year but still did not find the Electra.

Beginning in 1989, aviator Ric Gillespie began a series of expeditions to Gardner Island (now Nikumaroro Island) in search of evidence of Earhart, Noonan, or the Electra. Since that time, Gillespie and the group he founded, The International Group for Historic Aircraft Recovery (TIGHAR), have made ten expeditions to the island searching for clues that the Electra could have landed there. In 2001, Gillespie took a photograph of the island's coral reef at low tide, demonstrating that a plane could have landed on the flat area. TIGHAR has uncovered various artifacts but none have been proven related to the Earhart flight.

TIGHAR

Gillespie founded The International Group for Historic Aircraft Recovery (TIGHAR) in 1985. Three years later, he launched TIGHAR's investigation of the Earhart flight. Since then, Gillespie has led numerous expeditions to the Phoenix Islands in search of clues.

In an effort to solve the mystery of the disappearance of Earhart, Gillespie has collected all of the available documents related to the flight, pieced them together, and analyzed them for clues and evidence. These include official and unofficial logs and records of the event. The result is Gillespie's book, *Finding Amelia*. But even Gillespie's thorough investigation has left no clear answers.

Chapter 8

Where Is She?

In the decades since Earhart and Noonan went missing, their fate has remained a mystery. As biographer Doris Rich explained, "No one has been able to prove beyond a doubt how, why, where, and when Amelia Earhart disappeared. Records have been examined again and again, expeditions made, and theories expounded in magazine articles, books, and lectures."[1] But none of these has conclusively answered what happened over the Pacific that July.

The majority of these theories have formed around the idea that the Electra was lost or ran out of fuel and then crashed. The crash has been blamed on radio problems, instrument failure, or a failure on the part of Earhart or Noonan. Theorists speculate the plane went down either at sea or on a deserted island. After an exhaustive study of all the available records related to the Electra's final flight, Gillespie concluded of the missing plane, "As in most aviation accidents, the loss was not due to a single

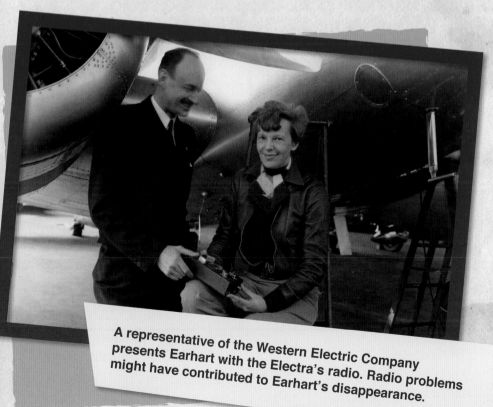

A representative of the Western Electric Company presents Earhart with the Electra's radio. Radio problems might have contributed to Earhart's disappearance.

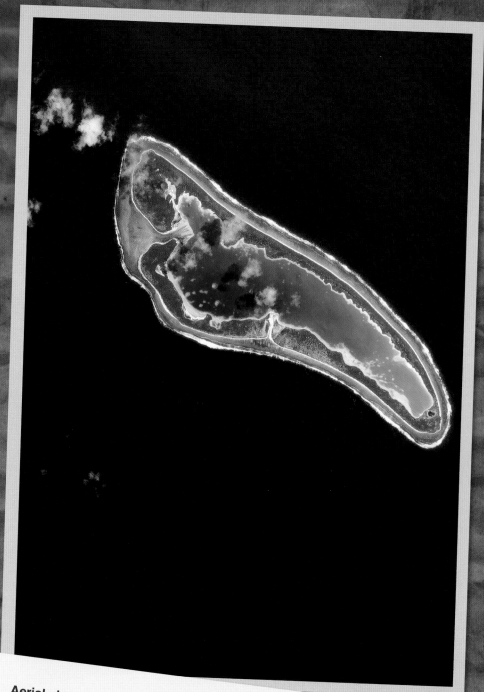

Aerial view of Gardner Island, now called Nikumaroro

catastrophic event, but rather the snowballing of a number of mishaps and errors."[3]

Clues

Despite searches of both the ocean and surrounding islands, little has surfaced to solve the mystery, to prove whether the Electra landed or crashed, or to understand where or what happened afterward. One bit of possible evidence emerged in 1940 in a telegram from Gerald B. Gallagher, officer-in-charge of the Phoenix Islands settlement, to the commissioner of the Gilbert and Ellis Islands.

The message explained, "Some months ago, working party on Gardner discovered human skull—this was buried and I only recently heard about it. Thorough search has now produced more bones (including lower jaw) part of a shoe a bottle and a sextant box."[4] The skull appeared to be that of a woman. The telegram continued, "Bones look more than four years old to me but there seems to be very slight chance that this may be the remains of Amelia Earhardt [sic]."[5] The bones were analyzed and measured in Fiji but subsequently lost. TIGHAR compared the 1940 measurements to photos of Earhart and Noonan but found no conclusive evidence the skull matched either of them.

More recently, a 2010 expedition to Nikumaroro Island (formerly Gardner Island) unearthed three bone fragments and some old makeup. The bones were tested for DNA to determine if they were human and, if so, if there was any connection to Earhart or Noonan. However, the results were inconclusive. Had these kinds of tests been available in 1940, when the skull and other bones were found, it is possible the mystery would have been solved. But as of now, none of the scant evidence discovered in and around Gardner Island has been linked to the Electra's last flight.

Other improvements in technology bring

Conspiracy Theories

Conspiracy theories have also arisen, speculating that Earhart and Noonan were on a spy mission for the US government and were possibly captured by Japanese forces. At the time, President Roosevelt vehemently denied these claims, and none of them have been substantiated since. In addition, Japanese historian Masataka Chihaya has declared it impossible for the Japanese forces to have captured the pilot and navigator; their planes at that time were not large enough, and the naval vessel said to have carried the Japanese planes was not in the area during the days surrounding their disappearance. The idea that Earhart was on a spy mission seems implausible at best; given the level of mismanagement of her world flight and her own history as an adventurer, it seems clear she was as she seemed— an amateur seeking excitement and lasting fame.

hope that new clues will be found. In April 2011, robots were used to scour the ocean floor in search of the wreckage from an Air France plane that went down two years earlier. A similar search might help find plane wreckage from Earhart's flight. Nauticos and the Waitt Institute have both developed technologies specifically related to searching the sea for the Electra.

Those interested in trying to find out more about what happened to Earhart have studied records of the time, interviewed people who were involved, and made expeditions to sites where either the plane or Earhart's and Noonan's remains might be found. Investigating this mystery involves learning as much as possible about the final days of the journey and trying to piece together the narrative of what might have happened to Earhart and Noonan in their final hours.

Earhart was a woman ahead of her time. She went on great adventures, fully aware of the risks, because it was fun and because she strongly believed that women were as fully capable as men. She was a pilot and a pacifist, an independent woman who provided for her family, a supportive colleague and friend, and a daring adventurer with an independent mind. Her legacy, and the mystery of her final

Women Flyers

Earhart was an early proponent of equal rights and thought women should be allowed to do anything men could do. Throughout her life, she supported her female colleagues, helping other women flyers to find funds or gain attention. In 1929, she was instrumental in founding the Ninety-Nines, an international group of women aviators still in existence today, and she served as its first president in 1931.

days, has inspired authors and filmmakers and has surely left an imprint on anyone with dreams as broad as the sky and as deep as the sea.

Amelia Earhart lived a life of "shining adventures."[6]

Tools and Clues

Tools and Clues Used in 1937

airplane design— Understanding the capabilities of the Electra, such as fuel use and flight speed, helped rescuers try to piece together where it might have landed.

direction finders— Both high and low frequency direction finders, which operate on radio waves, were in place to try to locate the Electra in the sky as it approached Howland Island.

Earhart's radio signals— Radio operators listening to Earhart's transmissions noted that they were difficult to hear and lacked information about the plane's location. Amateur radio operators picked up signals they believed to be Earhart's.

exhaustion and illness— Earhart flew for at least 19 hours straight and was likely ill as well. Fatigue could have caused her to make errors in navigation or in judgment.

missing antenna— A photo shows a missing antenna on the bottom of the plane, leading rescuers to piece together that she had difficulty with her radio.

radio equipment— The Radio Room aboard the *Itasca* was filled with state-of-the art radio equipment to transmit and receive messages with both voice transmission and Morse code.

Modern Tools and Clues

DNA Testing— Bones found by TIGHAR on Nikumaroro Island in 2010 were tested for DNA to determine if they could have belonged to Earhart or Noonan.

expeditions— Since 1989, TIGHAR has organized ten expeditions to Nikumaroro Island in search of clues that might help solve the mystery of the Earhart disappearance.

reconstructed flight path— Elgen Long interviewed people involved with Earhart's flight and conducted other research to reconstruct Earhart's route between Lae to Howland.

sonar and imaging systems— Nauticos and the Waitt Institute designed specialized sonar that could search underwater in their attempts to find wreckage from the Earhart plane.

underwater vehicles— Since 1994, four groups have used underwater vehicles to search around the area where Earhart disappeared but these have been inconclusive in solving the mystery.

PACIFIC OCEAN

Howland Island (US)

Baker Island (US)

Proposed route

KIRIBATI

PAPUA NEW GUINEA

Lae

SOLOMON ISLANDS

TUVALU

SAMOA

VANUATU

FIJI

NEW CALEDONIA

TONGA

N

Timeline

1897   Amelia Mary Earhart is born in Atchison, Kansas, on July 24.

1917   In Toronto, Canada, Earhart becomes a nurse's aide and becomes enthusiastic about flight while watching the military planes fly.

1920   Earhart takes her first trip in an airplane on December 28.

1921   Earhart takes her first flying lessons from Neta Snook at Kinner Air Field in Los Angeles, California.

1922   Earhart gets her first plane as a gift from her mother, a yellow Airster named *Canary*.

1923 In May, Earhart receives her international pilot's license from the Fédération Aéronautique Internationale.

1928 Earhart becomes the first woman to fly across the Atlantic Ocean when she lands in Wales on June 18.

1929 The Ninety-Nines hold their first meeting in November. Earhart was instrumental in starting this first women's flight association.

1931 Earhart marries George Putnam on February 7.

1932 Earhart becomes the first woman to fly solo across the Atlantic on May 20.

1933 On June 8, Earhart breaks her own transcontinental speed record.

1937 Earhart crashes her plane on the runway in Honolulu, Hawaii, in March.

Timeline

1937   On June 1, Earhart sets off from the Miami, Florida, airport with navigator Fred Noonan to begin her flight around the world.

1937   Earhart and Noonan arrive in Africa on June 8.

1937   Earhart and Noonan fly across the Red Sea and the Arabian Sea to land in Karachi, Pakistan, on June 15.

1937   Earhart and Noonan set off for Howland Island on June 30.

1937   The US Coast Guard and the US Navy search for Earhart and Noonan from July 3 to July 19.

1940   Bones found on Nikumaroro Island possibly
        belonging to Earhart or Noonan are analyzed
        and measured but subsequently lost.

1989   Ric Gillespie begins leading expeditions to
        Nikumaroro Island in search of evidence of
        Earhart.

1994   Dana Timmer leads an ocean search for
        Earhart's plane.

2002   Long and the Nauticos exploration
        company use sonar to scan the seafloor.

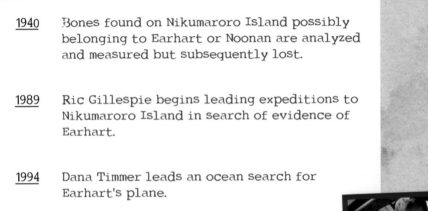

2010   Bone fragments are found on Nikumaroro
        Island. DNA tests are inconclusive
        and cannot determine if the bones are
        human.

Glossary

aerobatics .... Tricks performed on an airplane during flight.

aeronautics .... The science of operating aircraft and of flight.

aviator .... A person that pilots or operates any kind of aircraft, specifically an airplane.

chronometer .... A specialized type of clock with exceptional accuracy.

Coast Guard . . . . A division of the military or navy that guards or protects coastlines or waters in and around the coast.

Morse code . . . . A type of language developed to communicate across distances using a system of signals made up of dots and dashes.

publicist. . . . . Someone that works to bring attention and attract public interest to an event, act, or person.

solo. . . . . Alone.

taxi. . . . . To drive a plane on a runway.

telegraph . . . . A system for communication over long distances in which messages or codes are passed by electronic transmission.

wing-walking . . . . . . Stepping out onto the wing of a flying plane.

Additional Resources

Selected Bibliography

Gillespie, Ric. *Finding Amelia.* Annapolis, MD: Naval Institute Press, 2006. Print.

Rich, Doris L. *Amelia Earhart: A Biography.* Washington, DC: Smithsonian, 2010. Print.

Winters, Kathleen C. *Amelia Earhart: The Turbulent Life of an American Icon.* New York: Palgrave MacMillan, 2010. Print.

Further Readings

Fleming, Candace. *Amelia Lost: The Life and Disappearance of Amelia Earhart.* New York: Schwartz & Wade, 2011. Print.

Jerome, Kate Boehm. *Who Was Amelia Earhart?* New York: Grosset & Dunlap, 2002. Print.

Stone, Tanya Lee. *Amelia Earhart.* New York: DK, 2007. Print.

Web Links

To learn more about Amelia Earhart, visit ABDO Publishing Company online at **www.abdopublishing.com**. Web sites about Amelia Earhart are featured on our Book Links page. These links are routinely monitored and updated to provide the most current information available.

Places to Visit

Amelia Earhart Birthplace Museum
223 North Terrace Street
Atchison, KS 66002
913-367-4217
http://www.ameliaearhartmuseum.org/
This museum features exhibits about Earhart's life.

Museum of Flight
9404 East Marginal Way S
Seattle, WA 98108-4097
206-764-5720
http://www.museumofflight.org/
This museum features exhibits about the history of flight and space exploration.

Smithsonian National Air and Space Museum
Independence Ave at Sixth Street, SW
Washington, DC 20560
202-633-2214
http://www.nasm.si.edu/
The Smithsonian National Air and Space Museum features exhibits of historic air- and spacecraft, including the Apollo 11 command module and the *Spirit of Saint Louis*, Charles Lindbergh's airplane.

Source Notes

Chapter 1. Scanning the Sky

1. Ric Gillespie. *Finding Amelia.* Annapolis, MD: Naval Institute Press, 2006. 87.

2. Ibid.

Chapter 2. A Girl Born to Fly

1. Doris L. Rich. *Amelia Earhart: A Biography.* Washington, DC: Smithsonian, 2010. 6.

2. Ibid. 4–5.

Chapter 3. An Adventurer's Life

1. Doris L. Rich. *Amelia Earhart: A Biography.* Washington, DC: Smithsonian, 2010. 23–24.

2. Ibid. 36.

3. Ibid. 43.

4. Kathleen C. Winters. *Amelia Earhart: The Turbulent Life of an American Icon.* New York: Palgrave MacMillan, 2010. 53.

Chapter 4. Around the World

1. Kathleen C. Winters. *Amelia Earhart: The Turbulent Life of an American Icon.* New York: Palgrave MacMillan, 2010. 170.

2. Doris L. Rich. *Amelia Earhart: A Biography.* Washington, DC: Smithsonian, 2010. 221.

3. Ric Gillespie. *Finding Amelia.* Annapolis, MD: Naval Institute Press, 2006. 7.

4. Ibid.

Chapter 5. The Final Journey

1. Doris L. Rich. *Amelia Earhart: A Biography.* Washington, DC: Smithsonian, 2010. 242–243.

2. Kathleen C. Winters. *Amelia Earhart: The Turbulent Life of an American Icon.* New York: Palgrave MacMillan, 2010. 189.

3. Ibid. 192.

4. Ric Gillespie. *Finding Amelia.* Annapolis, MD: Naval Institute Press, 2006. 38.

5. Ibid. 41.

6. Doris L. Rich. *Amelia Earhart: A Biography.* Washington, DC: Smithsonian, 2010. 257.

7. Ric Gillespie. *Finding Amelia.* Annapolis, MD: Naval Institute Press, 2006. 43.

8. Doris L. Rich. *Amelia Earhart: A Biography.* Washington, DC: Smithsonian, 2010. 261.

9. Kathleen C. Winters. *Amelia Earhart: The Turbulent Life of an American Icon.* New York: Palgrave MacMillan, 2010. 205.

Chapter 6. Searching for Earhart

1. Kathleen C. Winters. *Amelia Earhart: The Turbulent Life of an American Icon.* New York: Palgrave MacMillan, 2010. 206.

2. Ric Gillespie. *Finding Amelia.* Annapolis, MD: Naval Institute Press, 2006. 109.

3. Ibid. 93–94.

4. Ibid. 108.

5. Ibid. 105.

6. Ibid. 108–109.

7. Ibid. 93.

8. Ibid. 172.

9. Ibid.

10. Ibid. 178.

11. Ibid. 182–183.

12. Kathleen C. Winters. *Amelia Earhart: The Turbulent Life of an American Icon.* New York: Palgrave MacMillan, 2010. 212–213.

Chapter 7. Theories and Possibilities

1. Doris L. Rich. *Amelia Earhart: A Biography.* Washington, DC: Smithsonian, 2010. 270.

2. Ric Gillespie. *Finding Amelia.* Annapolis, MD: Naval Institute Press, 2006. 122.

3. Kathleen C. Winters. *Amelia Earhart: The Turbulent Life of an American Icon.* New York: Palgrave MacMillan, 2010. 198–199.

4. Ric Gillespie. *Finding Amelia.* Annapolis, MD: Naval Institute Press, 2006. 103.

5. Ibid. 102.

6. Ibid. 206.

7. Ibid. 207.

Chapter 8. <u>Where is She?</u>

1. Doris L. Rich. *Amelia Earhart: A Biography.* Washington, DC: Smithsonian, 2010. 272.

2. Kathleen C. Winters. *Amelia Earhart: The Turbulent Life of an American Icon.* New York: Palgrave MacMillan, 2010. 214–215.

3. Ric Gillespie. *Finding Amelia.* Annapolis, MD: Naval Institute Press, 2006. 103.

4. Ibid. 241.

5. Ibid.

6. Kathleen C. Winters. *Amelia Earhart: The Turbulent Life of an American Icon.* New York: Palgrave MacMillan, 2010. 214.

Index

About the Author

A. M. Buckley is an artist, writer, and teacher based in Los Angeles. She is the author of more than 20 nonfiction books for children and adolescents, including the *Kids Yoga Deck* and *Once Upon a Time: Creative Writing Fun for Kids*.

About the Content Consultant

David Jourdan is the founder and president of Nauticos, an ocean exploration company. He is a graduate of the US Naval Academy and holds a master's degree in applied physics from Johns Hopkins University. He is the author of two books about ocean exploration, including *The Deep Sea Search for Amelia Earhart*.

Photo Credits